WHEN 2 BECOMES 1

MICHAEL & TANYA HARPER

When Two Become One

Michael & Tanya Harper

Copyright © 2024 Trient Press

All rights reserved. No portion of this publication may be reproduced, distributed, or transmitted in any form or by any means, including photocopying, recording, or other electronic or mechanical methods, without the prior written permission of the publisher. This restriction excludes brief quotations utilized in critical reviews and certain other noncommercial usages as permitted by copyright law. For permission inquiries, direct correspondence to the publisher, marked 'Attention: Permissions Coordinator,' at the following address:

Trient Press

5470 Kietzke Lane Suite 300 - #394

Reno, NV 89511

Criminal copyright infringement, including instances without financial gain, is subject to investigation by the FBI and incurs penalties of up to five years in federal imprisonment and a fine of $250,000.

Excepting the original narrative material authored by Michael & Tanya Harper, all songs, song titles, and lyrics cited within The Wealth Architect: Building Your Business and Personal Finances remain the exclusive property of their respective artists, songwriters, and copyright holders.

Ordering Information:

For quantity sales, Trient Press offers special discounts to corporations, associations, and other organizations. For detailed information, contact the publisher at the address provided above.

For orders by U.S. trade bookstores and wholesalers, please reach out to Trient Press at Tel: (775) 996-3844, or visit www.trientpress.com.

Printed in the United States of America

Publisher's Cataloging-in-Publication Data

Harper, Michael & Tanya

When Two Become One

Paperback: ISBN 979-8-88990-186-0

E-Book: 979-8-88990-187-7

Dedication.......

*This book is dedicated to
Michael Quentin Harper*

February 26, 1959 - June 15, 2021

Table of Contents.......

Introduction
Different Yet Familiar
Love and Logic
Honeymoon and Hostility
Husband and Wife
Blockades and Blessings
Planting and Harvesting
Slump and Recovery
Bittersweet and Sweetened Bitter .
Mistakes and Reflection
Never and Forever
Doubts and Confidence
Appreciation and Expression
Growth and Stagnation
Resistance and Positivity
Loyalty and Leverage
Complexity and Management
Patience and Communication

Pessimism and Optimism
Epilogue
About The Authors

Introduction.......

There are two ways to grow and prosper: Make mistakes and learn or learn from others' mistakes. Since there is only so much time in a single life, one can maximize his or her growth by simply learning from the remarkable journeys of others. While it may not be the humblest thing to assert, it is accurate enough to profess: our journey has been a remarkable one. And if you stick around for twenty chapters, I guarantee that you will learn a lot about communication, persistence, and time management.

This is the story of the Harpers. I'm Tanya Harper, and I present the collective takes of our household as I chronicle our journey from meeting each other to having our ups and downs and finally finding equilibrium. If you've had relationships where you found more than you loved each other, chances are this book will help you a lot.

If you have faced surprising circumstances where you had to improvise the best solution, you will relate to our struggle. More importantly, you'll find inspiration in our journey and end up with actionable steps that will help you in your love life, social life, and finances.

You may be thinking, "Well, I don't have such struggles." In that case, it is even more important for you to read this book because prevention is better than cure. Our story is one that involves sudden incidents that shook our lives. And by understanding how you can navigate your own life if it gets similarly affected in the future, you'll be in a better position to combat life's uncertainty.

In this book, you'll learn about how two individuals who were poles apart managed to meet, fall in love, survive financial problems, medical issues, and personality differences. You can read the entire book in one sitting or use it as a reference guide. Throughout the book, hold consistent the theme of polarity and duality. You'll notice that all chapters are titled with two highlights except the introduction and the epilogue, which contrast each other and are thus a duo.

That is because Mr. Harper and I are a duo that is similar in certain aspects yet different in others. And the dance where similarity amplifies love while differences spark interesting conversations is what one would call an ideal relationship.

This isn't a story about ideal people building an ideal household. It's about two humans with their individual flaws and personal obstacles getting over whatever stood in the way of their happiness. We aren't perfect; we're happy. And now, our mission is to use our story as the means to minimize misery. We truly believe that by reading the rest of this book, you'll find a shorter route to your personal happiness.

Different Yet Similar.......

Mr. Harper and I did not grow up together, and a part of me is quite glad we did not. It is all about timings: while we are perfect for each other, the way we have lived our lives has made us that kind of perfect within this relationship. Since this book is not about our individual stories, I'll not detail my past or his. Still, our past plays a big role in how we have navigated the challenges we faced together. And that's why at least a brief overview of our individual pasts is worth presenting.

Mr. Harper is a veteran and therefore has military discipline and strong will. But military life can make one obsessive in their pursuits. And when he got involved with drugs, this supposed advantage turned into quite a disadvantage. Fortunately, he understood that he needed to recover. And in the process, he found me.

I grew up in a family where my mom had the final say. Whatever she said went undisputed, and while I learned to respect her authority, I understood that it was conditional. I remember telling myself that the moment I don't need her, I will not listen to her or anyone. And in this rebellious lash back, I turned to my vices.

Growing up, I had adopted people-pleasing attitudes as a way to find love. I had some serious judgments regarding what I was doing to survive. And at a point in my life, I concluded that I wasn't worthy of love unless I was giving something. That's when I met Mr. Harper, and he taught me otherwise.

We were different in certain aspects: he didn't have the kind of family I did; his family was supportive. And I never experienced the life he lived to become a veteran. He came to Martinsburg to recover from his drug addiction. In his estimation, changing his environment drastically would help with his drug problem. He wanted to be away from the stimuli and influences of his past.

His move was from VA rehab in 2007, while mine was more of an independently directed move. I can't name a single reason I should have moved here and not to another place. But I had a million reasons to move away from where I was. In hindsight, I was always meant to move to Martinsburg first. I wanted to start a new chapter in the story of my life. Little did I know that this chapter was going to turn into a whole book.

Love and Logic.......

I was quite active in my church and, as a musician, would take up any opportunity given to perform. Mr. Harper, too, had his musical interests, as mentioned in the previous chapter. At a fateful time during our lives, this would bring us together.

There were two plays I was starring as the lead. And in one of them, an actor was supposed to play my husband. For some reason, four different actors fell through because of other plans, inability to show up to the practice sessions, or some other reason.

Mr. Harper got a role as a security guard in the play, and as the people who were supposed to play my husband couldn't show up, he got the bigger role. He, too, got sick, but unlike other actors, he kept showing up for rehearsals and powered through the performance. They say life imitates art, and that was certainly true for us.

He played my husband on stage before becoming my husband in real life. However, the transition from stage to real life wasn't as smooth. Mr. Harper wasn't the type to immediately fall in love, and I did not have the mind to open up to anyone. However, we had so much in common that we couldn't help but be in each other's company.

He had a past with substance problems, and I, too, had a past of battling my own issues. We took different approaches to get sober but had that in common. We were both trying to stay clean and counted each other as our positive influences.

One day Mr. Harper told me that his best friend's sibling had passed away. Since he didn't grow up in Martinsburg, his best friend was back home. I volunteered to drive him, and on that trip, we felt like we had known each other forever. There was a strong connection between the both of us, but I hadn't seen it as anything romantic.

I still remember the night we went out to have Chinese cuisine and got a fortune cookie at the end of our meals. When I broke open mine, it said, "your love is sitting right across the table from you." That was the first time I really considered it.

Initially, I had my reservations; he was too old for me, and in his mind, I was too young for him. But when I thought about it without my judgments regarding age, our connection with each other didn't have a gap. That trip and that meal would be the catalysts that switched our dynamic from a platonic one to a romantic one. We started getting closer now with romantic ends in mind.

Our previous "logic" would dictate against the relationship but how we felt was undeniable. There will be instances in your life where you may have to choose between love and logic. Some people will tell you love is better, while others will say you should side with logic. All I will say that whatever you pick is what you should be prepared for. Both choices will lead to their respective hardships, but in mine, I am glad I had Mr. Harper with me.

Honeymoon and Hostility.......

I hadn't really seen myself worthy of love without there being some sort of an exchange. This is the classic case of a people-pleaser. If you're reading this book, I advise you to stop and think up five things you can do to please yourself. Suppose you can come up with five activities that bring you pleasure without making someone else happy, congratulations you're not an obligate people pleaser. But if you have to do things like give away sweets, bake cakes for others, and serve others in any other manner to derive pleasure, chances are you too had a childhood where you weren't loved just for being yourself.

When people grow up having to please others to get attention, they develop a sense of self-worth attached to service. And as good as serving others is, it is toxic when done at the cost of one's own well-being. During the time I met Mr. Harper, I was still recovering from the effects of being a people pleaser.

The problem with being a people pleaser is that not everyone is worth pleasing: some people realize that you are a giver and try to take all they can. I had a fair share of those people in my past and was very defensive. I had my walls up and was cautious about what I gave, in terms of emotions and love, to others. But because I was holding back my service and emotions, I felt like nobody would love me just for existing. That concept was so foreign till Mr. Harper came along.

He made me feel loved, and there were days I would discover the heights of his admiration and feelings for me that I was previously unaware of. Then came the day where I discovered yet another height. We were in a Christmas play together in 2013. It was December 20th, and for some reason, my sister and mom walked onto the stage. That was quite sweet; I realized I was given a surprise reunion.

But as I turned around, I noticed Mr. Harper on one knee. Oh my God, was that really happening? "Tanya, will you marry me?" he asked. And I said "yes" without hesitation; there was nothing I wanted to do more. So, December 20th, 2013, ended up being the date we got officially engaged.

We stayed engaged for about six months before getting married in the June of next year. This period was that of testing the waters of mutual decision-making and strategizing regarding the future. As I mentioned earlier, I had my walls up. While I did bring the defenses down enough to get married to Mr. Harper, I kept the loud, rebellious nature of someone being forcefully domesticated.

I had too many ideas regarding married life that I was resisting. Mr. Harper didn't want me to be a certain way, but he had his own baggage. We both had anger issues and little patience for dealing with anti-compatible behavior. At the same time, we would rather be together despite our problems than be alone without them. And that is what initially kept us together.

Husband and Wife.......

We are influenced by stories, and for the longest time, outdated stories and tales that don't match our experience have been pushed down our throats. There are no Cinderella stories in my world. I would wholeheartedly reject a man trying to come into my life as the answer to all my problems because solving our problems is an exercise of freedom. If someone hands me the solution, he has ownership over me.

Initially, I was resistant to that idea, but Mr. Harper wasn't trying to be that guy. The other kind of story that has been generationally passed down is that the man is the sole breadwinner of the family, and Mr. Harper didn't fit that trope. That caused him to feel a certain way.

As we weren't open with our emotions, in the beginning, the relationship got rocky. In the three years since our marriage, we said "I'm out" quite a few times, but I'm glad neither of us meant it. I had an upbringing where I had to fight for my personal interests, and when you're in a unit with someone, you can't have that "me. vs. you" mentality. Mr. Harper was in the military, so he understood how valuable it was to think of "us" above "me." But because of how I acted, he got antagonized and solidified in his "me" positions.

When we got married, the social security decision-makers took him off his check because I was earning too much for the household by their standards. For context, I must clarify that working to earn $20 per hour is enough to get your spouse off their benefits. When Mr. Harper gave that up for me, I understood that it wasn't me vs. him; it was us vs. the world.

Now things were going to be easier. Or so I thought. Once he gave up his benefits, I tried to get another job that would pay more. That job ended up disappearing due to a hiring freeze. When I returned to my old job, I had to accept a pay cut. And that was more than 50% in pay-cut. I went from earning twenty dollars an hour to earning eight. Now there were more expenses and fewer dollars flowing in. It was like the moment we decided it was us against the world; the world came after us with all the problems it could muster.

Though that, we kept up two things: I used my gifts and interest in cooking to help those around me, and Mr. Harper used his military discipline and ability to drive to plant better in the community as well. Even though there were times when we were behind on the rent, I fed people around us, and he went around driving people at 5 am for Spiritual Warriors, an organization that fights drug use. The way we supported the community from our engagement to our marriage and afterward materialized in unexpected returns eventually.

In fact, a lot of our honeymoon was bankrolled by the community as we got an all-expenses-paid trip to Atlantic City and gift cards, among other things. We had $3000 in cash to ease our burdens as well. In hindsight, our married life started with extreme highs and lows, and it accelerated us to an equilibrium where now we understand each other very well and have a smooth relationship.

Blockades and Blessings.......

One thing is for certain: even during testing times, you'll have a share of your blessings, and it sometimes takes shocking incidents for you to realize the value of what you had. I, for one, had a partner I really cared about, someone who loved me for who I was. He had a supportive partner willing to do backbreaking work for extended hours to support our household.

But we also had financial limitations that kept us on edge. I've realized that so much relationship drama has to do with finances that one must attend a business coach's sessions more than relationship counseling. When you get your money right, a lot of your relationship problems disappear.

That said, I'm glad we had our initial money problems. That's because couples that don't face financial worries don't get to test their own character. My partner and I got to see ourselves when we had our backs against the wall. We fell behind on rent but were there for each other. I worked forty hours and then took additional work of equivalent length.

Aside from putting in 80 hours at work, I was also active in my studies, as was Mr. Harper. We barely had time together, and when we did, there were certain issues that would repeatedly rear their heads.

As my mother had the final say when I was growing up, I learned to be okay with conveying my disapproval in silence. For a relationship, this can have disastrous consequences. But this behavior was only amplified in my previous relationships where I was made to feel bad for expressing vulnerability or trying to communicate that I was upset.

So, when I was with Mr. Harper, I would try to go silent when I had something to say. He would then probe me to get me to communicate. "I'm fine," I would say. Often, he would reply with, "what do you mean by 'I am fine'? I can clearly see from your face that you are not."

During some group sessions, he would volunteer an answer on my behalf and put me on the spot. "Tanya has something to say," he would proclaim and then turn around and look at me intently. I had no idea what to do. The logical thing to do was to simply say what was on my mind. As we started communicating more, our relationship troubles started to tone down.

Through it all, we got elevated to church elder position together. We were active in the community, and Mr. Harper was quite passionate about combating drug use in the community. I was very skeptical of the sessions' effects on me as I had found my sobriety without such methods. However, through him, I discovered their value. We did so much good with no expectations of return that when we got blessed, I had no idea what to say.

I remember checking the mail once and then running back in. "Merry Christmas!" I exclaimed to a surprised Mr. Harper. "What do you mean 'Merry Christmas?' It isn't Christmas." he inquired. I beamed at him, "We got a three-thousand-dollar check.

Planting and Harvest.......

I have recently come to learn that one of the best ways to get rewarded by life is to plant better in life. Interestingly enough, when I look back, I see plenty of examples where we were the embodiment of planting better.

As mentioned earlier, Mr. Harper used to drive people for various positive organizations and groups, and we didn't just plant better for others; we improved ourselves as well. Education remained a priority during the toughest of times.

But now that we see where it has gotten us, our hearts are filled with gratitude. We never faked happy faces during our relationship troubles. And today, our happy faces are a genuine reflection of our happy life as a couple, as Christians, and as human beings.

When I brought Mr. Harper the news of the three-thousand-dollar check in our mail, he was as surprised as I. I remember asking him, do you know of the university that's paying you to study? He said he had no idea he had money coming in from there. That money eased a lot of our troubles.

At a point in our life, we weren't just behind on rent; our car had broken down too. As you know, a car can be an asset and a liability. If you go broke, but your car is fine, you can drive people around and earn a bit. However, if your car breaks down and you're broke, you need even more money to fix it.

But through such hardships, we learn to persevere. Alongside this, we also learn to focus on our problems and may miss out on being grateful for what we have. And that I believe I was guilty of. I had not truly appreciated Mr. Harper and his company till I got a wake-up call. I still remember it as if it was yesterday. I was with Mr. Harper, and we were watching a funny movie.

He, too, remembers it; one of the jokes was about being arrested for being ugly. This was around February second as it was his sister's birthday.

We were getting ready to go out for her birthday dinner when he suffered a stroke. I remember rushing in to see he was unable to speak. His sister and I both have medical experience, with her being a nurse and myself a CNA. We both knew something was wrong immediately because we could tell the signs of a stroke.

I suddenly had a pit in my stomach: was I going to lose him? I had only recently come out of my shell for someone. Why was this happening to me? I couldn't afford to get my heart broken. How would I take care of him? I was getting overwhelmed emotionally, so I bottled it all up, and we hurried him to the hospital.

Slump and Recovery.......

The stroke that Mr. Harper suffered in 2018 is undoubtedly the first steep slump of our relationship. I often say that I love him, but since we went through it, I love him differently. And a lot of it had to do with how we came together through it but also with the possibility of losing him.

I still smile when I think of how immediately after the stroke, Mr. Harper was ready to head out for the birthday dinner. He has quite the spirit. But thankfully, his sister and I both insisted he go to the hospital. Praying in the moment had helped him return to his senses, but if you don't get correct care right away, there are consequences that may linger.

For a whole month, he was in recovery. It started with blood-thinners. They said he had thick blood and possible clots. In other words, had we skipped taking him to the hospital, he may have suffered subsequent strokes. And in hindsight making the right decision was a blessing.

If we go back in my life and remove my CNA training and move the stroke to a day where his sister wasn't around, we would have just prayed it off, and Mr.

Harper would have remained vulnerable to yet another stroke.

So even though it wasn't obvious at first, the stroke occurring in the presence of two women with a medical background was a blessing in disguise. I didn't get into my feelings about it and believe that was quite a mistake. Thankfully, Mr. Harper recovered in just over a month.

They put him in rehab with strenuous therapy, and his strong will got him out in thirty days. This is the same will that kept him on stage despite being ill when we first met. It is interesting to see a man's character stay consistent when so much else around him has changed.

After 30 days of physical therapy, he was ready to be at home. Soon after, he was up and running. In about three months, he was back to work. He actually focused on all his faculties in recovery. From walking to speaking and writing, he practiced everything, and I stood by him through it.

Thinking whether he was going to be like that forever. I was supporting him, sure, but it was overwhelming. You must realize that this was four years into a marriage that had its shaky moments. But during this process, I began loving him more. Mr. Harper, too, was wondering why this was happening to us. Aside from the physical challenges, we realized that many "friends" were only there because we could help them. When we needed help, a significant portion of our circle disappeared. This, too, is a blessing because only a few of us truly find out who our true friends are.

Bittersweet and Sweetened Bitter.......

When we lived in Martinsburg, our first home was on Bittersweet lane. I believe the name was apt because our life was bittersweet. The landlord, however, was very nice. He would bring us food every now and then. That's always a pleasant surprise. Mr. Harper once said that he reminds him of us. And that is quite true. Just like I was eager to fix a plate for anyone who needed a meal, our landlord seemed to take pleasure in serving.

But that was also the place where every blessing seemed to have an air of melancholy. Our accomplishments seemed to go hand in hand with our trials. The peak of bittersweetness was when Mr. Harper was recovering. I was blessed to have him return to his healthier self, but at the same time, the tribulations kept mounting.

In hindsight, it is easier to have perspective and be grateful that fake friends left, but when that exodus was happening, it was infuriating. When you help people, and they prove to have only been your friends to get help, you cannot help but be disappointed.

Sometimes talking to people helps ease one's burden, but I couldn't even talk to everyone because not everyone is ready to listen. So many people see it as complaining when a friend is only seeking comfort. Others would just judge you before listening to you.

Needless to say, I felt alone. Harper had the burden of negative emotion as well. He, too, was wondering why he was being tested. And in this, we both kept each other up. I was at the hospital before it opened and sometimes would have dinner with him. There was so much uncertainty in the future.

was the church, and we were both studying as well. This kind of overload can break many marriages, but it also helps us be stronger. That's the thing about "make or break" periods; if they don't break you, they sure make you strong enough to survive the next one.

ittersweet lane, and that also helped us distance ourselves from past memories. The landlord passed away, and that was where bittersweet lane just became bitter. While we could have stayed there longer, the landlord's daughter was literally the opposite of her dad. She was nowhere near as understanding and wasn't service-oriented. That's why we ended up moving out of there but not before our second trial.

Mistakes and Reflection.......

By 2019, we were in a better position financially. We had more time to ourselves and could even think of a trip. But Mr. Harper got sick, so I had to improvise that plan. Instead of going as a couple, I was going to go and return to my husband shortly after. He wanted me to go alone as well because he had caught the flu. This was that period of 2019 where almost everyone had flu-like symptoms, and we can't be sure it wasn't COVID-19.

In hindsight, him not going was the best option, and I'm glad we took that. But when I returned, I noticed that he hadn't shaken off the "flu." So, we went to the hospital. You see, the flu doesn't really affect your ability to walk. That's why it made sense when the doctors said he had pneumonia. But now, I had to re-think my initial suppression of emotions.

Remember how I mentioned that I had bottled up my emotions regarding losing him? Well, this was seeming like a second round of that with consequences higher in severity. While his previous issue was to do with thinner blood now, it seemed like his body had higher WBCs.

The term WBC stands for White Blood Cells, and these are responsible for fighting infections, among other harm-causing factors. If one's body has a high WBC count, there's something the body is combating. The density of WBCs in Mr. Harper's blood didn't make sense for pneumonia, so there had to be another thing.

When the doctors pondered the fact that he had trouble walking, they narrowed their attention to his legs. Upon removing a sock, we knew immediately what the problem was. We could smell the infection: there was a visible spot on his heel.

I must preface this by saying that this had not been there when I left for my trip because he's diabetic, and I check him regularly for scars or other problems. S,o while I was away, he had developed an infection that needed to be cut out. Doctors even hinted at requiring to cut off the leg altogether.

This made no sense because what is the point of removing an infection from the heel if you're going to take the leg off? It was obvious that the doctors wanted an easy way out. Mr. Harper denied giving consent for such a procedure. His stance was that if the Lord was going to take him, then it was his time, but he wasn't going to lose his legs in the process.

They sent in six different doctors to test their persuasion. Mr. Harper asked, "why are you sending new doctors when my answer isn't going to change?" At that point, one of the doctors said, "you will not make it to 2020; you'll be dead in 2 weeks."

Hearing that immediately sent me into the bottle where I had suppressed all my emotions. There was no way I was going to lose Mr. Harper. I wanted to backhand the doctor, but a part of me wanted to convince my husband to get his leg cut off if that meant we could be together. Little did I know this was only the beginning of our troubles.

Never and Forever.......

I had said I was never going to do certain things in life. Cleaning up after a man was for sure something I wasn't going to do. But when I was with Mr. Harper as he was going through it, the "He vs. Me" dynamic just melted away. It was us vs. the world. And that's where we became truly close. Mr. Harper stuck to his guns and refused to have his leg amputated. The doctor who tried to scare us into making that decision was in the wrong.

I am glad that we have both made it to 2021 alive and well. But I would love to take this moment as the turning point in our relationship. And in the story of our lives, we can contrast it with who we were initially.

Take Mr. Harper, for instance; coming from a military background; he wasn't going to lean on a woman to support him. He was a proud individual who had previously dealt with all his problems solo and just powered through everything. Now he was in a vulnerable position and relied on me and the doctors to survive.

in the washroom would have seemed antithetical to my identity. But I guess love is all about finding that person who makes you want to overcome your limitations. The limitations of service I had imposed on myself went away when the end goal was to help my husband survive.

He was in hospice for a whole year, and we had a sudden move sneak upon us. It was like our problems were compounding, but one this was different: us. We were now better prepared to handle challenges that would have broken us up in 2014. They wanted to separate us since he was in hospice and I was moving, but with the right demands, we managed to stay together.

We lived in a hotel, and they moved his hospital bed to the hotel. That allowed us to be together. You can contrast that with the initial attitude I had prior to 2014, and you would not believe that being with Mr. Harper was that important to me. Yet, I am glad for this transformation as it set us up for what was to come.

We have since found financial stability. In fact, our move had us doubting our finances because I had pretty much no money. That was their rationale for suggesting that Mr. Harper stays in hospice while I moved away. This comes full circle to what I mentioned in my introductory chapters: a lot of relationship problems are financial problems. And that is why I was determined to improve my finances from that point onward.

Doubts and Confidence.......

We've reached the halfway point of the story of the Harpers. That's why it's only apt that we reflect on how our doubts turned into confidence through sheer faith and persistence. It is our hope that the book doesn't just tell our story but also gives you actionable lessons and inspires you to power through those moments of instability.

Financial doubts

When you're in a hole from the financial standpoint, you're likely to multiply the present with the rest of your life. One of the most painful views to hold is that your current pain is perpetual. Looking back at how we became financially stable, it seems laughable that I ever worried about how our short-term finances will impact us over the long run.

Most people sit with their doubts and let themselves be weighed down because of said doubts. I don't believe that is healthy. The best way to shut out doubts is to jump into action. I jumped into action when my income got cut in half, and Mr. Harper lost his benefits.

At one point, I was working 40 hours a week and then working the same amount in additional hours just to make ends meet. Had I thought this is how life would be forever, I might have gotten demotivated. However, I had faith that our condition would change. I want you to make a note of that as well. Whenever you're in financial trouble, have faith that over the long-term, things will get better if you do whatever it takes to take care of yourself now.

Relationship doubts

We had certain preconceived notions regarding each other, and we're not the only ones who do. Humans, in general, come to a relationship with the baggage of ideas. Even in your first relationship, you bring expectations set up by your parents or others whose relationships you have observed in person or on TV.

The doubts I had became the trap that wouldn't let my relationships blossom. I had assumed that the man would try to oppress me, and I wasn't going to submit to anyone's will. But that defensiveness is what pushed my partner to be vocal about his interests making the entire relationship a perpetual shouting match.

If you are a strong-willed individual, I must warn you that your individualism could be detrimental to your social life. I recommend observing yourself with a critical eye and distance. Ask yourself if you would date yourself had you met "you" as a third party. If not, you need to fix your attitude.

People can be a product of their circumstances but don't have to be. We are the prime example of the fact that you can change if you want to. We didn't just change for the better; we also steered ourselves to a better future. But if you resist all change, you reject all opportunities for growth. Change is inevitable, but if you're intentional about it, at least you have a chance at making it work for you instead of becoming a victim of its circumstances.

Appreciation and Expression.......

The second key lesson from our journey so far is that appreciation and expression are linked. If you appreciate someone, you must begin by expressing this to yourself. I hadn't fully acknowledged how important Mr. Harper was to me till he had a stroke. They say we take our blessings for granted until they're taken from us. While that is okay to do with material things, you should never do that with people.

If you do not feel grateful for your money or your house, you may lose it but can always get it back. However, if you lose another human being, the chances of getting them back are pretty slim. So please appreciate those you cannot afford to lose. More importantly, express it to them.

The world is so critical, and we communicate whatever we're displeased with: why do you leave your tower like that? Why do you shut the door like that? It goes on and on. But when's the last time you told your partner what you appreciate about them?

I believe that whatever we count is what we're essentially seeking. And you get what you seek. If you'll look for reasons to be annoyed by your partner, trust me, you'll find them. But if you look for reasons to appreciate them, you'll find those as well.

Compared to our initial years, we're in a much better place in terms of romance and domestic understanding. However, we still have our disputes and disagreements. The problem is assuming that these disagreements should not occur. If you believe that, you'll take every argument personally.

In no relationship is one partner a carbon copy of the other. If we had enjoyed our own company so much, we wouldn't need a partner in the first place. It is boring to have a partner who just agrees with you on everything. So be appreciative of disagreements because they signify individuality. They display your partner's autonomy.

Even if your partner disagrees with you on many things, they still believe that you're worth loving. Ultimately that should matter more than anything. With that said, I understand that there are relationships that are extremely skewed in the other direction. If you don't voice what's bothering you, you'll build up resentment, and it will cause an explosion with unfair consequences for your relationship.

As I mentioned earlier, I grew up in a household where my opinions weren't given enough attention. As a result, I had learned to be okay with being silently bothered. Thankfully, Mr. Harper put in the effort to pull these opinions out of me.

You may not have a Mr. Harper in your life to do this for you. In such a situation, you must be your own Mr. Harper. Put yourself on the spot, so you have to voice what is bothering you. You can't expect your partner or friends to read your mind. That's an unrealistic expectation. As you know, unrealistic expectations lead to disappointment. It is also possible that you may need to play Mr. Harper's role for your partner if they've grown up in circumstances similar to mine. In any case, please make sure expression remains a priority in your household.

Growth and Stagnation.......

Everyone talks about ups and downs, yet rarely does the concept of plateaus get brought up. Plateaus are as important as growth spurts because they help you consolidate your growth. In our lives, we have gone through periods of growth. For instance, Mr. Harper discovering the VA support group was one such turning point in his life. Joining the church was a similar moment for me.

Coming together was again an exercise in growth. And while I worked over time, I was growing financially. But I had not yet grasped the concept of plateaus. A plateau is where you get to enjoy how far you have come. In my opinion, there is no point in growing if you don't find it rewarding.

To constantly feel inadequate and pursue the next level can be torturous. If you're reading this book, we're sure you are interested in personal development. And if that's the case, you better learn to enjoy your growth during your consolidation stages.

Stagnation vs. Plateau

We're writing this book during a period of consolidation as we harvest the fruits of what we have planted. Plateaus prepare you for future growth, and we have signed up for exciting opportunities to grow our brand, amplify our message and help our community. The reason we emphasize the importance of plateaus is that they often get disregarded because of their connotations with stagnation.

Stagnation is not the same as a plateau. A plateau is equivalent to a period of peace in a war-ridden world. Before you conquer your next milestone, you strategize in the moments of calmness. On the other hand, stagnation is aimless surrender to one's circumstances.

Respect Time

There is a time for everything, including growth and rest. Learn to respect time so you can acknowledge the season you're in. A lot of our frustrations arose from not knowing which season of our lives we were in.

I've made it a point to mention that we met at the right season. Had we met before, we would have butted heads and been so annoyed with each other; we'd barely be friends, let alone partners.

However, we stayed single in our love-live plateau. I improved myself while Mr. Harper worked on himself. And when the time was right, God sent us into each other's lives. Now imagine how different things would have had we both insisted on finding a partner a year prior to finding each other.

Therefore, finding each other is in part due to us accepting our respective plateau of solitude. Please remember that if things aren't going up in your life right now, it might very well be because your plate needs to be empty for what's about to come. Your perspective shapes reality to a certain degree, and slumping your shoulders and seeing your plateau as a negative will turn the plateau into a pathway for stagnation.

Persistence and Positivity.......

Mr. Harper and I have built irrational persistence in the face of life's challenges, and that's the secret to our improving conditions. If you're in a place in life where every step you take forward seems to take you back two steps, you must read this chapter with a lot of attention. It sums up some of the most important lessons we learned in our journey.

Don't over-analyze failures

It is healthy to learn from your failures, and usually, we have been advised to analyze our role in the problems that plague us. But in my experience, blaming yourself while exaggerating a bad situation will not help you get out of a slump. We kept wondering why we were going through the painful times when Mr. Harper suffered, and I was dealing with the possibility of losing him.

I spent a good deal of time thinking about whether I would have to take care of him for a long time. A rude doctor even predicted Mr. Harper's death in two weeks' time just to manipulate us into giving consent for an easier, albeit inessential, procedure. Mr. Harper stood his ground because he had a positive outlook on the future.

The first lesson then is to rely on positive faith instead of negative analysis when you're in a slump. Remember that your negative emotion is emphasized disproportionately, which means all the "logic" that you're processing is tinted with negative bias. That is why you should avoid over-analyzing your circumstances.

Focus on the solution

One of the most rewarding questions you can ask yourself is, "what can I do to make things better?" Mr. Harper and I fought a lot initially because we both had our ideas regarding what the other could do to make things better. For instance, he wanted me to be more vocal. Only thinking about how I would say nothing and insist I would frustrate him. But things changed. Mr. Harper asked himself what he could do to facilitate communication between us. The answer he came up with was brilliant.

He started putting me on the spot where I had to express myself. I've made a note of instances where he volunteered answers on my behalf. He would tell the group that Tanya had something to say. When everyone expected an answer, I did say what was on my mind. Here you can see the value of switching the question from "what can she do differently" to "what can I do to make things different?"

Similarly, I was seriously disappointed with my pay-cut, but instead of over-analyzing that or asking myself how the world should be different for things to be fairer for me, I asked myself what I could do. And the answer was to work 80 hours a week. I didn't question its possibility or sustainability; I just got to work. Long story short, now I don't have to work even half as much to be financially free and spend my time doing things I love, all thanks to persistence and positivity.

Loyalty and Leverage.......

Before we explore our story further, there's one final lesson we would like to emphasize: loyalty isn't an obligate virtue. Yes, it is great to be loyal to the right person, but if you are too generous with your loyalty, you may end up with core wounds that keep you from being loyal to the right person.

This was a close call in my relationship with Mr. Harper. Previously, I had been stung every time I was loyal to a man. And that had led me to get stingy with my loyalty. In hindsight, if I were initially stingy with my loyalty, I would have been clearer in my thinking and would have let down my guard around Mr. Harper. This would have saved us a lot of energy which we exerted due to friction.

Another thing to keep in mind is that your loyalty is not likely to be reciprocated. In other words, don't expect others to be loyal to you just because you would have been loyal to them. Assuming loyalty will only lead to heartbreak.

If you do good in your community, make sure your expectations don't sneak up. Do good with no ulterior motives in mind. Mr. Harper and I are passionate about the causes we champion. We have not thought about returns for a second and have been sufficiently blessed by our surroundings. However, during our toughest times, watching our "friends" disappear was disappointing.

That is why it is not enough to avoid expecting things. To avoid being disappointed, you should mentally prepare yourself for a significant number of your friends not showing up at the moment you need them the most. With this perspective, you won't be disappointed when people bail on you. More importantly, you'll be grateful for when friends actually show up for you.

Mr. Harper's family is a military family; he grew up with the unit supporting him. To this day, they all come together when one member of the family is in need. My family experience wasn't even close to this. Despite having grown up with people who supported him, Mr. Harper took it well when our "friends" disappeared around the time he was facing medical complications. This underscores the importance of actively managing your expectations.

If you are a couple, make sure at least one of you has a more realistic opinion of people and their willingness to help. Above all, you should both work to be in a position where you don't have to rely on others. That's the best place to be in life. When you can help each other out, and the community around you comes together to help even though you can survive without them, your overall life experience is much more wholesome.

Complexity and Management.......

I personally struggled with the sudden complexity of the situation. If you're facing a sudden incident, tragedy, or unpleasant situation, do your best to simplify it such that it does not overwhelm you. Defeat occurs in mind. Your brain is powerful and ultimately controls your body. Going by the adage that humans have infinite potential, one would suggest that you can overcome any challenge. But that can't happen if your focus is scattered.

I wasted a lot of my energy getting emotional about how people weren't helping. Of course, it affected me because things would have been slightly easier had some people been a little more selfless. But practically speaking, getting angry about that wasn't helping anyone. The first step to reducing a situation's complexity is to eliminate everything that should not be draining your energy.

This can include emotional activity like reflecting on the past or actual physical tasks you need to stop doing because they aren't productive. The next step is to execute the ones you have to. And here I aced.

I powered through the long work hours and other supporting activities. I wish I had help, but even in its absence, I got my part done. I am glad Mr. Harper's encouragement and love were there to constantly encourage me to push myself. But you don't have to do it all alone. So, make sure you know who you can rely on. There will be moments where you really won't be able to rely on anyone, but please don't manufacture those moments for yourself. IF you can delegate tasks, please do.

In fact, it was quite frustrating for Mr. Harper when he couldn't do everything by himself. He's a proud man and also older than me. Yet, I am happy he did not make things tougher by making it a point of contention. Ultimately, it comes down to what brings about a better flow.

There will be times when things will flow better when you delegate tasks to employees, friends, and partners. Other times that will cause friction and drama, and you really should do everything by yourself. IF you choose to do everything by yourself, though, please avoid the fallacy of equality in priorities. Not all tasks have the same value. Some will matter more than others, and your attention should first go to what is necessary and then to what is not as essential.

Finally, avoid doing anything that you can get away with not doing. It might sound wrong, but it is a favor to yourself. In challenging times, conserving your energy is important, and therefore you should only do things you can't afford not to do. For me, these were: working for our income, taking care of Mr. Harper, and making sure the household chores were handled. In hindsight, I could have paused studies and church and managed to get through the period with relative ease, but I did not know what I know now. Now I am better at managing complexity and handling problems.

Patience and Communication.......

As Mr. Harper was coming back to his complete communication faculties, I had to cultivate a lot of patience. And in that process, I learned that patience and communication go hand in hand. Initially, he would try to express his thoughts in a sentence but would have trouble finding a word. I would try to help by guessing the word, and this would frustrate Mr. Harper. My gut instinct was to come up with another word or suggestion. However, Mr. Harper's frustration wasn't that my guesses were wrong, but it was due to the fact that I was trying to take away his necessary struggle. I want to emphasize, therefore, that you should be careful which problems you take off someone's plate because sometimes we need to battle certain demons to become better people.

I soon learned to curb my people-pleasing behavior of trying to bail Mr. Harper out of his predicament. With sheer willpower, he improved his expression to the degree where he can now communicate his ideas without anyone jumping in. While knowing this will help you most directly if you're taking care of a patient who has suffered a stroke, you can use this information in your dealing with anyone who is developing a particular skill.

If you are a parent, don't try to make things easier than they should be for your kids. Many parents with good intentions baby-proof the world for their kids. When your children don't know how money works because they get everything they want, you're interfering with their ability to develop the desire to earn, just like I was interfering with Mr. Harper's ability to regain his ability to communicate. It happens out of love but isn't ideal for the people we love. Instead, you should have the patience to see them get stronger.

This doesn't apply just to kids. It also applies to students. These could be your actual students or friends you're mentoring in something you're good at. You might have such a high standard of perfection in mind that you may want to butt in and tweak whatever they are working on. Again, you have to ask yourself what you prioritize: perfection or their development?

For a significant part of 2018, Mr. Harper wasn't communicating in a way that was easy for me to understand but ultimately, I valued his journey more than my convenience. In your relationship, you must always remember that if you're together only because it is convenient, you'll break up when it gets inconvenient. You must prioritize the other person and their well-being over your convenience.

Pessimism and Optimism.......

As we come closer to the conclusion of this book, I would like to address one change that has made the biggest impact on our relationship: moving away from pessimism. Mr. Harper is a natural optimist, and one would think that being in the company of one automatically makes you more open to optimism. That's not the case. In fact, your partner being perpetually optimistic can antagonize you and make you more pessimistic.

Remember that there is no such thing as being realistic. To an optimist, optimism is realism. To a pessimist, pessimism is realism. And since I was more open to analyzing negative possibilities, I thought that I should look at the downsides for the both of us because he was too optimistic. He likewise had his own reservations regarding my perpetual pessimism. But his attempts to convince me to see the brighter side never amounted to anything because I wasn't going to "let a man change me." This goes back to my initial defensiveness.

However, around 2018, things got so painful that I had no option but to see the bright side. I gave that a try and haven't looked back since. In this chapter, I want to make a case for optimism by highlighting three key benefits it holds.

Optimism clears up mental space

When you see problems from a pessimistic lens, you're using a lot of your brainpower to find out why things won't work out. Needless to say, this isn't very productive. More importantly, this processing power could have been used to actually solve the problem. When you see things more positively, it frees you up emotionally and mentally. You're better equipped to solve your immediate problems.

Gets rid of communication errors

We've made it a point to emphasize the importance of communication in a relationship. Still, it is impossible to communicate everything all the time. So many things get left unsaid. You don't know about your partners or intentions at all times. But if you assume the positive possibility regarding their intentions, you will have fewer arguments. IF they say something that hurt you, you will assume they didn't mean to inflict pain, but if you're a pessimist, you'll take it personally because you'll lean towards the negative possibility.

Optimism improves life experience

Our experience of our lives is subjective. They say that on the deathbed, people recall the peaks and valleys of their lives: the high points and the low points. That means the person who focused and remembered the positive will conclude he lived a happy life, whereas the pessimist might depart this world thinking his life was bad despite living through the same circumstances as an optimist.

That said, my natural openness to negative emotion is something I have to fight actively. Please don't judge yourself if you naturally adopt a pessimistic outlook. Our openness to negative emotion is largely biological and judging yourself for being negative is also a negative thing to do. Simply allow yourself to let go of the initial negative outlook that emerges and consciously reinterpret things to be more positive.

Epilogue.......

You have read the story of our beginning. This book chronicles the beginning of the Harpers' and the empire they aspire to build. Yes, all the struggle we went through was the equivalent of a kid graduating from school. He cannot, in all honesty, say that the conclusion of his school years is the end of his story. Similarly, what we have learned in the six years since we got married has only built the foundation for what we will do next.

You may see our names all over the news media, or you may not hear of us again. The future for us is open, and we'll decide what success means to us and go for it. Personally, I have always found fulfillment in helping people. Mr. Harper, too, is quite passionate about his community work.

Writing this book is just the first step in scaling our impact. This book helps make a positive difference in the world even when we're sleeping. That Idea intrigues me, and I will research other ways to scale our positive impact. This book will be like a time capsule when we look at it five to ten years from now. It is written in a period where we have found out happiness and see an infinite number of doors open ahead of us. For us, this is no epilogue; it is only the prologue to the rest of our lives. I'm excited for what the future holds for us, and I hope you learn from this book and build a future you are excited about.

Much Love,
Tanya with Mr. Harper.

About The Authors.......

Tanya Harper was born in November in the Northern Virginia. She is the eldest girl of five other siblings.

She has received her Bachelor of Biblical Studies from the College of North Carolina of Theology in 2009. In 2019 she is completed her graduate degree in Biblical Studies as well. She holds certification as an nursing assistant and medical administrative assistant.

Harper had recommitted her life back to the Lord at a women service held in May 2005. She loves expressing the love of God through fellowship with others and music. She has traveled to foreign mission field in Panama and does local mission in the city with which she lives.

In October 2011 Tanya Harper started her own business Agape Hands Care Services. In June 7th 2014 she married Michael Harper. In August 2015 she wrote her first book "Releasing and receiving" book of poetry.

Michael Quentin Harper born and raised into a military family decided to follow in the footsteps of his parents Melvin & Doris Harper, who are now deceased, in serving his country. After graduating Dover Air Force Base High School in 1977, Michael enlisted in the United States Army and then later after serving in the Army went on to pursue his Military Career and enlisted in the United States Air Force. Michael's military assignments took him to various tours of duty both state side and overseas.

Michael is the father of two daughters and a son between the ages of 40 being the oldest and the youngest being 30. He is also a proud grandfather. He accepted Jesus just after the birth of his youngest child but backslid a few years later until he came to the Martinsburg VA Hospital center for drug rehabilitation program April 4th, 2007 where he rededicated his life to the Lord.

Michael has 14 years sober and chairs and attends Alcoholic Anonymous meetings regularly. Michael now serves as a mentor to other veterans and ministers the message of hope and deliverance to those who have lost their way. He carries a powerful testimony and fire of praise and worship which he attributes to being around his sister, Prophetess Debra Harper. Michael is affiliated as a committee board member with a **"Faith"** based Outreach Ministry in Martinsburg, WV entitled, "Spiritual Warriors."

This Ministry is an organization that ministers to the physical, spiritual and emotional needs of our nation's veterans. Spiritual Warriors is a group of veterans and nonveterans that meet at the VA Hospital Chapel, 6am to 7am, and 6 days a week to praise and worship the lord and also study God's word. He has been a facilitator of Spiritual Warriors for over 8 years and has been attending faithfully for over 10 years before getting sick in 2018.

Since graduating from the drug rehabilitation program at the VA hospital in 2007, Michael started playing the trumpet and was able to visit different churches where he testified about how Jesus has changed his life. Michael now lives his life in a way that glorifies God and is a blessing to his family and friends abroad. Every day he tries to exemplify the courage of a Warrior of God and strives daily to use his talents and gifts to help and encourage others. It is his mission and purpose to proclaim the Gospel of Jesus Christ and to tell others his personal experience with the healing, deliverance and keeping power of the almighty God that literally saved his life and delivered him from the streets of DC into the service of the Lord.

In 2014 Mike received his BA in Cyber Security. He also married Tanya Thorne in June 2014

www.ingramcontent.com/pod-product-compliance
Lightning Source LLC
LaVergne TN
LVHW030324070526
838199LV00069B/6555